COACHING & RE

P

By Peter Hook,
Ian McPhail &
Andy Vass

Cartoons:
Phil Hailstone

Published by:

Teachers' Pocketbooks
Laurel House, Station Approach,
Alresford, Hampshire SO24 9JH, UK
Tel: +44 (0)1962 735573
Fax: +44 (0)1962 733637
E-mail: sales@teacherspocketbooks.co.uk
Website: www.teacherspocketbooks.co.uk

*Teachers' Pocketbooks is an imprint of
Management Pocketbooks Ltd.*

Series Consultant: **Brin Best**.

© Peter Hook, Ian McPhail and
Andy Vass 2006.

This edition published 2006.
Reprinted 2007, 2008.

British Library Cataloguing-in-Publication
Data. A catalogue record for this book is
available from the British Library.

ISBN   978 1 903776 71 1

Design, typesetting and graphics by **Efex Ltd**.
Printed in UK

Contents

Foreword

Coaching is very much part of the language of education today. Strategies from the DfES and programmes from the National College for School Leadership reference and endorse coaching as a method of school improvement at all levels.

One of the reasons that coaching, as a development tool, fits so comfortably in schools is that it has a strong focus on individual learning. Also, because coaching is about holding high quality conversations it taps into the strong interpersonal skills that most teachers naturally demonstrate.

This book explores coaching as a specific set of skills that can be flexibly applied, whether you're doing the coaching or being coached, to help you:

- Connect to your strengths and feel valued as an individual
- Feel confident and supported
- Achieve goals which are relevant to you

Foreword

Schools today operate in a climate where continual improvement is an expectation. To achieve and be able to **sustain** improvements, they need to build increased personal capacity in teachers and children alike. In other words, they must **maximise potential**.

By definition coaching is about maximising potential. It seeks to develop people, helping them to become 'even better' and more 'consciously competent' in their roles.

Set within a relationship of trust and confidence, and having a focus on solutions and personal growth, coaching enables improvements in performance to be generated **internally** within the school and, therefore, to be easily shared with others. This is essentially what capacity building is.

Most schools would claim that people are our most important resource. Coaching offers one way of actually demonstrating that to be true.

Foreword

Because skilled coaching is largely about asking challenging and thought-provoking questions that lead towards positive outcomes, **coaching** and **reflecting** are **mutually supportive processes**.

Every teacher has examples from their own experience where the opportunity to discuss and reflect on their practice with colleagues has brought benefits, eg:

- Gaining a clearer perspective
- Resolving an issue of concern
- Exploring new ideas
- Feeling supported and affirmed in their practice
- Learning from other people's experience

In this book you will find several ground-breaking ideas to support you and your colleagues in reflective practice. You will also find that the coaching skills you gain from reading this book are equally effective in facilitating and adding value to the process of reflection.

Introduction

Begin with success in mind

We'd like to ask you a few questions because that's what coaches do. What happens when you imagine that this book is really useful to you? That it enhances your ability to hold influential and motivating conversations with colleagues, students and parents? That as a result of reading it now and dipping back in from time to time you become even more confident and even more effective in your work and maybe other areas of your life too?

How will you recognise that this is happening?
What are you doing differently that pleases you? What else?
Who will notice that things are different and even better?
What are they noticing? What else?
What do these positive changes tell you about yourself?

These are **solution-focused (SF)** coaching questions. They encourage you to think about future success. Our coaching approach in this book is solution focused.

What is coaching?

A definition which fits with our approach is:

> *'Unlocking a person's potential to maximise their performance. It is about helping them learn rather than teaching them.'*
>
> **John Whitmore.** (See reading recommendations, page 126.)

Coaching seeks to create change. The process of change begins with conversations. These conversations could be ones we have with ourselves (self-talk) or those with colleagues. Often they are a combination of the two. However, it is VERY difficult to ask yourself a question that you don't already know the answer to.

A skilled coach will ask you questions which respectfully challenge your thinking with the aim of helping you to set and achieve goals that help you become even better.

It is the skill of knowing how to ask the most useful question at the most appropriate time and in an empowering and thought-provoking way that distinguishes a really good coach.

What's in it for me?

Coaching, when skilfully and respectfully used, is a powerful learning experience. This is true whether you are coaching or being coached. Teachers who have been involved in coaching with us describe the benefits variously as:

- Thinking more clearly about things
- Feeling valued and listened to
- Recognising and appreciating their skills and resources
- Increasing their range of options
- Clarifying how they'd like things to be as they get even better
- Understanding what they need to do to get there
- Becoming more creative and optimistic
- Feeling more positive and confident about change

Importantly, high quality SF coaching will always place your agenda at the centre of the process making it empowering and motivational.

What's in it for me?

Case study

'Two years ago I was appointed deputy head of a school in extremely challenging circumstances. I had attended a conference on solution-focused coaching just prior to my new appointment and found the ideas a revelation, both in their simplicity and in the potency of their application to school improvement.

I read widely and received additional coach training so that I was not only coaching as an integral part of my role, but becoming confident enough in the knowledge and skills of SF coaching to lead training for other teachers. Although I had spent the previous five years working with challenging schools across an LA, this was a very different experience and one I approached with a radically altered philosophy.

In the past, when working with subject leaders to help them develop I was really quite directional. I was ready with well-intentioned advice backed up with modelling and then monitoring. It was a 'here's what you need to do and here's how you do it' model – efficient and effective but, ultimately, very one-sided and often short-term. Once the monitoring and support were removed, progress slowed down and occasionally ceased.

Case study (cont'd)

Since adopting the solution-focused coaching approach I have noticed a difference in the relationships I build and the confidence and independence with which colleagues who have been coached, rather than directed, approach their work.

I am currently coaching two new subject leaders in my school: an experienced core subject leader new to the school and a teacher experienced in the school but new to leading a core subject.

I have focused on asking questions with genuine curiosity rather than seeking to offer advice. Many of the questions have been challenging, requiring deep thought and reflection about the coachees' vision as effective subject leaders. I've been inquisitive about how their journeys will develop, encouraging them to fix milestones or steps to recognise their own success. I've also sought to really listen to gain a greater understanding of the strengths and resources they bring to their roles. As a coach, I need to encourage them to amplify the qualities that make them successful.

Case study (cont'd)

The benefits have been significant. My colleagues tell me they feel empowered and energised. Changes that have happened have been sustained because they've been built around strengths.

A recent Ofsted inspection placed us as outstanding across the board – a real tribute to everyone's skill and effort. Yet I'm convinced we can become even better: solution-focused approaches deepen and enrich our insights into how we are successful. Regular conversations throughout the school on our preferred future create a very strong collaborative state of mind. Actively focusing on the strengths and resources of all members of our community does wonders for motivation too.

For myself, SF coaching has improved me as a leader, a teacher and a learner. I'm more attentive to what people are really saying and I look for strengths in children, colleagues and parents that help us learn and develop successfully together.'

Karen Hirst, Richmond Primary School, Oldham.

Where can it be useful?

We cannot think of a single area of school improvement that cannot be enhanced by applying high quality coaching skills. In our work we have used coaching approaches to:

- Become even more influential and motivational as teachers
- Create strategic development plans
- Support troubled students at risk of exclusion
- Develop the Every Child Matters agenda within LAs
- Improve performance management dialogues
- Develop self-evaluation through the Excellence Model
- Build a common language to support culture change
- Develop high-performing leadership teams
- Build hope and optimism in schools in special measures
- Empower children in plenary sessions
- Create positive outcomes in challenging parental relationships

What isn't coaching?

Our preferred definition of coaching emphasises the process of learning.
Pure coaching is **non-directive**. It's helping people uncover their own solutions rather than giving advice, telling them what to do or solving problems for them. It sits comfortably with the way school agendas are shifting from teaching to learning.

However, schools are complex organisations and no one process or model is suitable in all contexts. Other types of supportive conversations exist and get labelled as coaching but do not fit our definition. We like to view those conversations as part of a continuum of support (see next page) rather than actual coaching.

The coaching continuum

A trainer should know more about the subject than the trainee, so that information is transferred and a potential skill or knowledge gap is filled. This is closest to the concept of sports coaching.

A mentor should have relevant and similar experiences to the person being mentored. Mentors act as models, offer advice, and provide reflective challenge. There are certain overlapping skills with coaching.

A coach does not need the knowledge base of the coachee. Coaches use questions to challenge thinking and promote reflection. They lead people to create their own personal solutions and seldom give direct advice. They hold the coachee accountable for taking actions to achieve their own goals.

A useful adage is: **trainers and mentors know lots of answers, while a coach knows most of the questions**.

Agreed roles

All of the activities along the coaching continuum can contribute to successful development. What matters is clear agreement between colleagues as to how they are best offered the support they want. It would be foolish to refuse to offer direct advice or to share knowledge and experience with an NQT just because it didn't 'fit' with a coaching definition!

Equally, if you wanted the opportunity to explore and reflect on your practice to find meaningful ways forward on an issue, the last thing you want is someone saying, *'What you need to do is…'*

The important thing is for the coach to maintain awareness of their **agreed** role within the school's approach to coaching and be sensitive to where on the continuum they are operating.

What is good coaching?

Good coaching:

- Is non-judgemental
- Is based on trust and respect
- Focuses on solutions
- Works to the coachee's agenda
- Emphasises strengths and resources
- Uses skilful questioning to challenge your thinking
- Involves strong empathy
- Involves deep listening
- Holds you accountable for your own goals

As well as characterising effective coaching, the above points embody the principles of a solution-focused approach.

A Solutions Focus

Changing conversations

We have established that coaching is about creating change. We also know that asking respectful but challenging questions triggers reflection, expands your perspectives and in this way supports the process of change. Effective coaching questions should lead the coachee to consider:

- **What** changes they want to make (personal goals and preferred future)
- **How** they can achieve the change (actions plus resources)
- **Why** they want the changes (benefits and motivation)

Coaching aims to support the coachee's journey towards finding solutions that are both meaningful and positive to them. The questions, therefore, must focus on future solutions rather than past or existing problems.

Feel the difference

Work with a colleague and take turns to ask each other the following sets
of questions:

- What is the problem?
- How long have you had it?
- Where does the fault lie?
- Who's most to blame?
- What's your worst experience of it?
- Why haven't you solved it?

- What do you want instead of the problem?
- How will you know when you've got this?
- What else will improve as a result?
- What resources do you already have to help?
- What is something similar you've achieved?
- What's the next step?

What were the differences for you between these sets of questions?
How did they feel different? What were the differences in responses they generated?

This is a really powerful illustration of how language links to emotion and
thought processes.

Solutions vs. problems

The questions on the previous page illustrate the difference between problem-centred and solution-focused thinking. Although there are many models of coaching, all **effective** coaching is solution focused.

In our experience the left-hand set of questions generates short, often one-word answers and feels uncomfortable. In contrast, the right-hand set opens up dialogues, creates possibilities, and very often leads to a way forward.

Exploring problems in great depth tends to leave people and organisations feeling frustrated. They simply end up knowing more about what doesn't work. It also generates a lot of negative energy and emotions which often lead to blame and impaired collaboration. Worse still, since the dialogues that occur are the foundation of a school's culture, problem-focused approaches inhibit high performance and are demotivating and disempowering.

Digging away at a problem simply makes the hole deeper!

Problem-focused thinking cycles

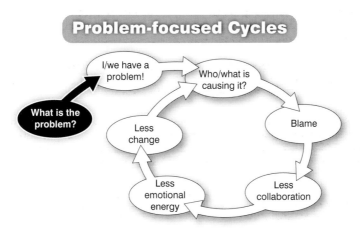

With thanks to Ben Furman and Evan George for the initial idea.

A more effective way

An SF approach acknowledges the reality of issues and difficulties and then presents a fundamental shift of emphasis. It asks questions like:

*What do you want **instead** of the problem?*
If this issue were (re)solved what would be different?
Imagine this team is being as successful as it can hope to be. What is that like?

In asking these and similar questions you orientate people's thinking towards:

* A solution – often called a **preferred future**
* Describing successful actions and attitudes
* Building positive expectations
* Opening up possibilities for change
* Focusing on resources to support change

Solution-focused thinking cycles

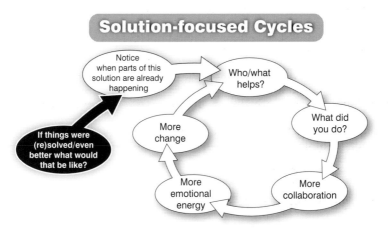

With thanks to Ben Furman and Evan George for the initial idea.

Coaching for solutions

Solution-focused coaching seeks to empower people to find their own
solutions through exploring and then amplifying their own strengths and skills.
It looks for examples of success, however slight, and encourages you to do more of
what works.

It is based on eight key principles:

1. Moving towards a solution is far more useful than moving away from a problem.
2. People are experts in their own world.
3. People have preferred futures.
4. People have a wealth of strengths and resources.
5. All problem patterns have exceptions (when it's better/more manageable, etc).

Coaching for solutions

6. Small changes in the right direction often lead to bigger changes.
7. Find what works and do more of it.
8. If it isn't working, stop doing it and do something differently.

It's a simple truth – if you amplify/do for longer/do in a different context your 'success behaviours', you *will* be more successful!

Case study

'Partly to explore the potential of the Teaching and Learning Responsibilities pay structure and partly because it was right for the school's development, we sought to move from having Heads of Year towards Learning Managers. The change was not cosmetic. We needed to create a change in thinking built on consensus in order to clarify new roles and responsibilities. It was essential that the relationship between SLT, Learning Managers, and Heads of Department was clear and mutually supportive.

During a staff residential course, Andy Vass introduced us to solution-focused thinking. It was energising to focus on and describe in detail our preferred future. This greatly increased our motivation for change. We also examined what is already working well and how we could extend and amplify that success.

The experience was infectious and increased the commitment of all staff to support the changes, which in turn has impacted positively on the pupils.'

Clive Howlett, Headteacher, Padgate High School.

Solution-focused Tools

Overview

To support and complement the range of general coaching skills described later in the book, solution-focused approaches draw on some distinct and very powerful additional tools:

1. **Exceptions** (pages 31-34)
2. **The Miracle Question** (page 35)
3. **Scaling** (pages 36-40)

Integrating these tools appropriately into general coaching and applying a solution-focused philosophy allows you to generate conversational shifts:

From	Towards
Deficit ➔	Resources
Complaint ➔	Preferred future
Being stuck ➔	Movement
What's wrong ➔	What's right
Resistance ➔	Collaboration
Anxiety ➔	Confidence
Limitation ➔	Possibility and potential

Exceptions

A solution-focused approach holds the view that no one does things consistently 100% of the time, including how they 'do' problems! **Exceptions** form the core of an SF approach.

Exceptions are those times when difficulties or challenges are:

- Absent
- Better
- Less intense
- Don't last as long
- Easier to manage

Exceptions

Another way of looking at this is that exceptions are examples (however small) of the preferred future, or something close to the preferred future, already happening.

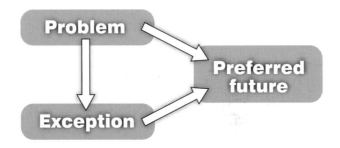

Exceptions

For a coach these exception times are significant as they:

- Often provide impetus to the process of change
- Move attention towards solutions
- Provide counter examples to problems
- Offer evidence that the preferred future is possible
- Tend to increase motivation and confidence
- Highlight behaviours or perceptions that are more valuable
- Focus on moments (however slight) of success

Once the coachee has begun to focus on these exception times, the coach can explore the **differences** between these and other less valuable times.

Exceptions – questions

- *'Tell me about the times when X happens less?'*
- *'What are the lessons/parts of the day when X bothers you least?'*
- *'What do you suppose keeps you from doing X more often?'*
- *'What is it you are doing when you are not doing X?'*
- *'Tell me about the last time that X seemed a bit more manageable?'*
- *'What are the times when X is less dominating?'*
- *'How come you sometimes resist the urge to X?'*
- *'What's the longest you've gone without letting X get to you? How did you do that?'*
- *'When things go wobbly/pear-shaped, etc how do you get things back in check?'*
- *'What's something you can tolerate about X and maybe even enjoy once in a while?'*
- *'How come you haven't given up on this?'*
- *'What things have people not noticed about you or you not noticed about yourself in these situations?'*
- *'Tell me about a time when the problem happened and you were able to get to grips with it better. What was different about that time?'*

Miracle question

Perhaps one of the best-known SF tools is the miracle question. In coaching it encourages the description of the coachee's preferred future. This question needs to be asked with curiosity and with pauses between the phrases to allow the person to engage with the spirit of the question.

'Imagine when you go to sleep tonight... a miracle happens ... and the difficulties you have been talking about disappear... As you were asleep you didn't know that the miracle had happened... When you wake up what would be the first signs that the miracle had happened?'

Conceptually, the question can be very powerful since it suggests clearly that obstacles to progress *have been* overcome, allowing the coachee to tap into their imagination freely and unimpeded.

Scaling

Scaling is a very versatile tool for coaches and can be applied to many contexts, eg: confidence, optimism, motivation, commitment, hope.

It involves asking a deceptively simple question:

'Imagine a scale running from 0 – 10 where 10 represents achieving your outcome or when you've reached your goal, and 0 is the opposite. Where are you right now?'

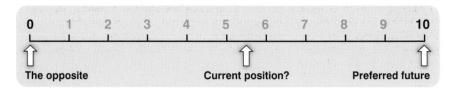

Scaling

The scale itself is totally subjective and therefore where a coachee places himself or herself is not important. However, by picking a number there is implicit acceptance that:

a. There is a 0 and a 10
b. Generally they will not be at either of those
c. Movement or change is therefore possible

You will notice coachees usually pause and reflect before offering a number. During this time they are weighing up their current situation and how they feel about it. Placing themselves on the scale represents an intuitive response given in quite a logical or linear way. This can be very useful where the coaching touches issues that have a strong emotional context.

It is also a 'safe' process because whatever the coachee says will be correct since it is their own internal representation.

Scaling and resource building

Whatever number on the scale a coachee chooses, there's an opportunity for directing their attention towards competence and resources.

Suppose level 5 is chosen, the coach can ask with curiosity:

'How come you gave yourself that number rather than zero?'

Your role as coach is then to help them develop their answers in detail, building up a detailed picture of:

- What is working well for them
- How they are tapping into these skills
- Who or what else is helpful or supportive

This brings very positive building blocks for progress into focus. It is common for motivation and commitment to increase as a result of these types of conversation. It is also highly likely that doing more of the things that got someone to 5 will get them to 6.

Scaling and resilience

When coachees place themselves quite low on the scale you can begin by orientating the conversation towards resources for coping and resilience. Ask questions that enquire how they:

* Got through or got by so far
* Stopped things getting even worse
* Still come to school every day!

Then, if appropriate, further details can be developed to build positive complimentary views about them as individuals.

'How did you manage that?'
'What does that say about you?'

Scaling and first steps

Coaching is about change and therefore a major part of the process is focused on taking actions that move the coachee towards their chosen goal.

Returning to the coachee's scale is a great platform for considering these action steps by asking: *'What would the next smallest step along the scale look like to you?'*

Then follow up with: *'What would you need to do to get to 6?'*

As coach you can encourage the coachee to build as detailed a picture as possible using developer questions such as *'What else?'* and also maintaining a focus on action, eg: *'How will you do that? What will that take?'*, etc.

Small changes

Focusing attention on the initial small steps that begin progress and change is certainly less risky and more likely to generate commitment. It also begins the process of movement from which the next steps emerge. Equally, small changes in the coachee's actions are likely to lead to altered responses from others such as colleagues or children.

Most teachers already have many experiences of this in action. Increasing our use of praise, looking more closely for the strengths of a child, differentiating tasks are all examples of making small changes that affect our interactions with others.

An SF coach will explore first steps with the coachee that:

- Involve doing more of what has already worked
- Have the best chance of success
- Can be done immediately
- Are within the influence of the coachee
- Are positive, ie things to do rather than stop doing

Case study

'As part of my NQT year I was fortunate to receive some coaching. I found the experience very empowering since I was encouraged to focus on issues that mattered to me. Being new to the job I felt my levels of assertiveness could improve. Following a lesson observation my coach gave me feedback about the tone of my voice in saying 'please' when I gave an instruction. After talking this through and exploring my options I decided to substitute 'thanks' for please which is an idea I had come across in some NQT training.

My coach and I role-played some scenarios until I had a clear idea how I would blend the words, tonality and posture together.

I have put this into my practice regularly since and I have been really surprised (pleasantly I might add) by the increased compliance of the children as a result.

Teaching is such a busy job that realistically you can only change a little at a time. This process has given me so much confidence in making small and manageable changes.'

AH, NQT in Hertfordshire.

Coaching Skills

Overview

The process of coaching differs from other professional conversations that occur in schools because it involves adopting a specific role and working within an established structure. At the simplest level, coaching involves:

Asking questions

Focused listening

Offering feedback

Pages 53-66 deal with each of these in turn.

While these skills are also common to the process of teaching, there is a more specific agenda in coaching which crucially belongs to the coachee. In meeting this agenda, most coaches work within a framework or structure. Pages 49-52 offer one such model.

The coach's role

A coach seeks to explore three questions in detail.

1. *'Where are things right now?'*
2. *'Where would you like to be?'*
3. *'What do you need to do to get there?'*

In coaching dialogues, as opposed to other types of professional conversations, the coach takes on a very specific role. It is characterised by:

- The balance between talking and listening – a coach does more of the latter
- The depth of listening that occurs
- Maintaining the focus on the coachee's goals
- The commitment to the coachee generating their own solutions
- A focus on creating action steps towards that solution
- Maintaining the integrity of the coaching process
- An acknowledgement by the coach that he/she doesn't have all the answers

Building rapport

Whatever coaching model or approach you take, it will be ineffective without the establishment of rapport with the coachee. Rapport is the essential connectivity that allows people to communicate openly and honestly with each other. It is usually a naturally occurring process in skilled teachers.

Think of a colleague you connect easily and comfortably with. That person is likely to:

- Listen well and demonstrate this by reflecting or summarising
- Not judge you, be open to and value your thoughts and ideas
- Offer non-verbal encouragement to develop your ideas
- Build trust by sharing and/or disclosing appropriate information about himself/herself
- Maintain confidentiality when requested
- Help you feel good by affirming and validating your skills
- Make time for you rather than 'fit you in' between lessons

To develop your coaching fully we strongly urge you to explore the skills of rapport-building in more detail. (See recommended reading, page 126.)

Building trust

A central feature of the coaching relationship is the degree to which the coachee believes the coach is honest, genuine and on their wavelength.

Building trust is a **process** rather than a 'one off' occasion. You earn trust by doing things that are trustworthy. For example:

- Demonstrating a belief in the coachee's resources and qualities
- Acknowledging that you do not have all the answers
- Allowing the coachee to set the direction of the dialogue
- Maintaining integrity by working within agreed protocols
- Keeping to your commitments within the coaching role

Equally, some simple practical elements support trust:

- Is the time allocated protected?
- Is the room private and quiet?
- Is there agreement about notes and confidentiality?

A coaching structure

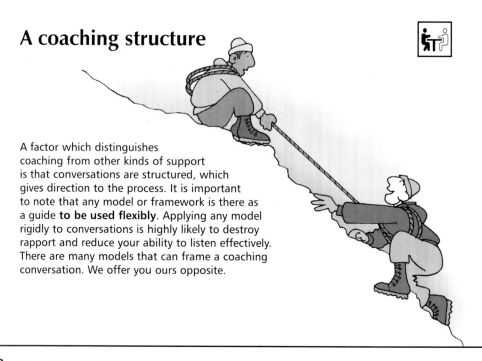

A factor which distinguishes
coaching from other kinds of support
is that conversations are structured, which
gives direction to the process. It is important
to note that any model or framework is there as
a guide **to be used flexibly**. Applying any model
rigidly to conversations is highly likely to destroy
rapport and reduce your ability to listen effectively.
There are many models that can frame a coaching
conversation. We offer you ours opposite.

The COACH approach

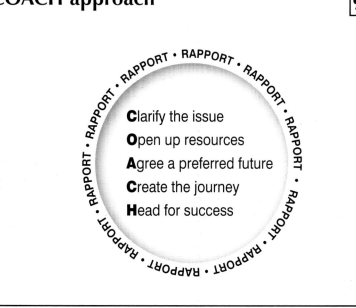

RAPPORT · RAPPORT · RAPPORT · RAPPORT · RAPPORT

Clarify the issue
Open up resources
Agree a preferred future
Create the journey
Head for success

The COACH approach

Clarify the issue

Use questions, reflective listening, scaling, and feedback to establish the current reality:

- *'What would it be useful for you to discuss in this session?'*
- *'Describe to me the issue from your perspective'*
- *'What are your thoughts about...?'*
- *'What's the main issue here for you?'*
- *'On a scale of 0-10 where are things right now?'*

Open up resources

Focus the coachee's attention on strengths and resources that may be useful and on exceptions (more successful times):

- *'Tell me about the last time this was more manageable'*
- *'What were you doing or thinking differently when it worked better?'*
- *'What's something similar that you've achieved in the past?'*
- *'What does achieving that tell you about yourself?'*
- *'I'm curious about how your past experiences in industry could be useful to you here?'*

The COACH approach

Agree a preferred future

Develop a core SF concept:
- *'What are your best hopes from this coaching session?'*
- *'When things are more like you want them to be, what will you be doing differently?'*
- *'What would it be like if things were even better?'*
- *'What do you want instead of the problem?'*
- *'Imagine being really successful in this venture. What is that like?'*

Create the journey

Focus the coachee on:
- *'What are your options for action to achieve your goal?'*
- *'Which strike you as most useful right now?'*
- *'What are your first steps?'*
- *'Who or what will be useful to you in this process?'*
- *'How will you recognise you've reached your goal?'*
- *'If you are 5 on your scale now, what does 6 involve?'*

The COACH approach

Head for success

Build detail around how the coachee will achieve their goal(s):

- *'How will you do that?'*
- *'What will that take?'*
- *'Who would notice that things had changed?'*
- *'What would be the first signs that things were moving in the right direction?'*
- *'What are the implications of making this goal happen?'*
- *'How will you maintain the necessary confidence and determination?'*
- *'How will you put the necessary support in place?'*
- *'How will you celebrate achieving your goal?'*

Using questions

Questions are the backbone of the coaching process and are used to:

- Acquire or check information
- Develop more detail
- Create reflection
- Expand perspectives
- Establish direction and goals
- Rehearse a future success

Constructing questions

Julie Starr, in her book *The Coaching Manual* (Prentice Hall, 2003), defines the characteristics of a great question as:

- Simple
- Having a purpose
- Influencing without being controlling

In our experience, a great question is usually followed by a short period of reflective silence. Welcome this as a coach rather than try to fill it as a teacher!

Starr goes on to present the benefits of effective questions as:

- Refocusing thoughts from problems to solutions
- Tapping into creativity and creating options
- Helping people feel powerful and constructive
- Making problems feel more like challenges or opportunities
- Creating forward movement, ie action towards goals

Developer questions

Because effective coaching questions challenge you to consider ideas in new
and different ways, you may find that the responses are, initially, at a superficial level.
Encouraging the coachee to expand and develop their answers using some of the
following 'prompts' can be useful.

'Go on'
'How did you do that?'
'What did that involve?'
'I'm curious about...'
'Tell me more about how you...?'
'What else?'
'What do you think...?'
'What would be your best guess about...?'
'In what ways was that helpful?'
'What did it take to sustain that approach/idea even for a short time?'

The more detailed the picture you build, the broader the perspective you obtain.

Example questions

Questions beginning with 'why' are often perceived to be judgemental or possibly accusatory. *Generally*, questions beginning with **'what'** or **'how'** form the basis of coaching questions.

* *'What do you want from this?'*
* *'What would be an action you could take to...?'*
* *'Can you describe to me...?'*
* *'How do you know?'*
* *'What's the real/main issue here for you?'*
* *'When was the last time that it was less troublesome for you?'*
* *'What factors contributed to that?'*
* *'I was interested that you said....What makes you say that?'*
* *'Can you explain the thinking behind that?'*
* *'What would be the first step towards this?'*
* *'How might this become action?'*
* *'How will you deal with that in a way that you feel comfortable with?'*
* *'What effect will that have?'*
* *'What could you do to....?'*
* *'What are your options?'*

Listening

Feeling listened to is, for most of us, a very satisfying state to be in. Within a coaching relationship it is an essential element.

Effective listening enables you as a coach to:

- Demonstrate commitment to the coachee
- Strengthen rapport
- Gather relevant information
- Develop an understanding of the coachee's world
- Affirm and value the coachee
- Support the idea that the coachee provides their own solutions

Importantly, listening to really understand what is being said also provides you with the information to frame your next question.

Levels of listening

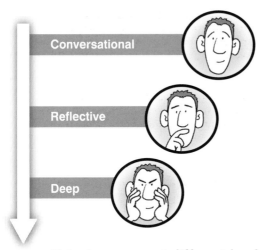

Conversational

Reflective

Deep

Listening occurs at different levels within conversations.

Levels of listening

Conversational listening involves alternating between listening and talking. It is not so essential that you take on board all the nuances being expressed. You also begin to match your own experiences of what the person is saying in order to contribute examples and experiences of your own. The balance of talking is often more evenly shared.

Reflective listening demands greater emphasis on the listener to tune in to and validate what is being said and the emotions associated with it. More focus is given to encouraging the other person to open up and develop their conversation. Specific skills are used such as:

* Verbal and non-verbal encouragement – nods, *'Uh huh'*, *'Go on'*
* Reflecting back and validating – *'So you felt let down when X happened'*
* Summarising – *'What we have discussed so far is…'*

Levels of listening

Deep listening requires that the listener be really 'present'. That is, your sole focus of attention is on the other person. You will need to close down your own internal dialogue and suspend judgement and opinion as you listen. It is often associated with a state of great calm.

Deep listening allows the listener greater insight into the other person's world. It is a powerful sense of seeing the world through their eyes. In this state, the subtleties of information which can be hidden in direct speech become more available and significant.

From the speaker's perspective there is a stronger sense of being understood and a strengthening of the trust and relationship.

Deep listening cannot generally be maintained for long periods as the coach will need to ask questions, check out assumptions, or provide validation, encouragement, or other feedback.

Coaching shifts between reflective and deep listening.

Silences

SF coaching questions are very powerful; they're not typical everyday conversational questions. Your coachee will need time and space to reflect and consider their answers. This is especially true when exploring ideas in more depth and developing insight/understanding around events.

For a teacher, perhaps the hardest element of coaching is to be comfortable with silences after asking a question. We tend to fill silences in class either by asking a subsequent question or by answering it ourselves!

Naturally, as a coach you need to be sensitive to the silences. The intention is to give the coachee thinking and reflection time rather than let them squirm to find an answer.

Case study

'As Head of REACH (Responding to Exceptional and Additional needs of CHildren), I lead a small team in North Lincolnshire supporting schools to address some very challenging situations that staff, children and families face every day. We were initially asked to look at schools and identify gaps in provision. Why were children sometimes fast-tracked to fixed-term exclusion, despite a wealth of expertise within the schools, the families, and other agencies who were all trying so hard to support their youngsters?

One of the team's strengths, which developed during our solution-focused coach training, was how to really listen. Listening to others, not offering what you think they want to hear, leaving the silence, waiting for them, letting them take their time to tell their story as they see, feel, and live it is what enables us to respond appropriately.

We listen with our ears, our eyes, our hearts and our undivided attention. We can then work with the strengths of the individuals we are privileged to be alongside. We can integrate our expertise with theirs as we support schools, children and families to move towards solutions rather than away from problems.'

Sheila Jennings, North Lincolnshire REACH Team.

Listening summary

- Talk less and listen more (remember you have two ears and one mouth)
- Demonstrate you are listening – reflect; summarise; use non-verbal signals
- Shut down your inner voice
- Be comfortable with silences – people need time and space to think
- Maintain full attention
- Let go of **your** solution to the issues presented
- Listen with the curiosity of a fascinated stranger
- Be aware of what **isn't** being said but avoid making assumptions

Giving feedback

Whilst giving feedback to someone does not constitute coaching, feedback, when it meets certain criteria, can add value to the coaching process. It is important to consider the differences between feedback and judgement or constructive criticism.

Within coaching, there is no such thing as 'constructive' criticism.

Feedback, effectively offered, can provide:

- Accurate information to compare points of view
- Prompts to encourage insight and reflective thinking
- Support in achieving goals
- Impetus for action
- Confidence and motivation

Criteria for feedback

Feedback should:

- Be factual and describe behaviours
- Be honest and accurate
- Focus on issues within the control of the coachee
- Have a positive intent and be sensitive
- Contribute to the coachee's learning

Feedback should not:

- Interrupt the flow of a conversation
- Be judgemental or critical
- Result in the coach becoming over controlling
- Be based on assumptions or prejudice

Feedback vs. judgement

Your goal, previously discussed with the coach, is to improve the quality of questioning. Consider your response to receiving these two pieces of feedback:

> **1.** 'The lesson was good overall. I think you handled the children well but I thought your questions were rather narrow and largely biased towards the boys.'

> **2.** 'In the opening phase of the lesson you asked the class 11 questions about the characteristics of living things. Five of the questions were closed questions and seven of the questions were answered by boys. What are your thoughts around that?'

In the second example, the coach offers objective feedback without judgement and then asks for the coachee's thoughts. This contributes to the coach remaining true to working with the coachee's agenda and is likely to trigger some reflective thought on the part of the coachee.

To be able to give factual and honest feedback, the tone of voice is crucial as is the relationship of trust and honesty developed between coach and coachee.

Offering opinion

Inevitably there will be occasions when the coachee requests an opinion from the coach. This does not necessarily mean the coach is obliged to give one.

Coachee: *'I can't make up my mind about going for this new post. What do you think? Should I apply?' Am I ready to be a Deputy Head?'*

Coach: *'What I'm really interested in is what you feel about it – what's your current thinking about this?'*

The coach avoids undue influence or 'leading' and refocuses the coachee on the decision that they have to take.

Of course, if **direct** requests for ideas or help are always avoided, this may reduce the trust and confidence of the coachee.

Giving advice whilst coaching

Some ways a coach may offer ideas and maintain a coaching perspective are:

1. Give examples from practice that parallel the current situation.
   'Some teachers find…'
2. *'This reminds me of a similar issue I/a colleague had. What helped there was…What do you think would be useful to you from that?'*
3. Give a range of possible options and allow the coachee to choose which they feel suits them best.

Role-play possible options so the coachee can 'try them on'.

General talk and compliments

Coaching isn't about interrogating the coachee or getting to the point as quickly as possible. General chat about the weekend, families, etc can all contribute to the rapport and often help normalise the process.

Paying compliments in a genuine, non-patronising manner is a much overlooked way of building very strong rapport with people. Although they can make some people feel awkward, we all actually like them.

The most effective compliments are a reworking of facts offered to you by the coachee and which affirm their positive characteristics. For example, if your coachee says they enjoy going to aerobics every week, a possible compliment would be:

'So you're pretty dedicated to staying in shape and taking care of yourself.'

Because the information came from the coachee but has been connected up to a positive attribute or quality, the coachee is highly likely not only to accept the compliment but potentially view themselves more positively.

Review

To recap, the skills of coaching involve:

- Building trust and rapport in an appropriate environment
- Accepting a specific role and working within a preferred structure
- Asking skilful questions
- Listening at different levels
- Offering supportive feedback
- Focusing attention on resources and skills, eg with compliments

A characteristic of the best coaches we have worked with is the desire they show to constantly develop, refine, and improve these skills. Within schools there are many everyday opportunities to use these skills both formally in coaching and in general teaching, management and leadership dialogues.

Introduction

 A Solutions
Focus

 Solution-
focused Tools

 Coaching Skills

 Setting Goals ◀

 Developing
Coaching in Your
Own School

 Reflective
Practitioner
Groups

 Further
Information

Setting Goals

Why goals?

Goals provide the key focus for a coaching conversation. They set the direction and provide the rationale for the coaching relationship. Remember that the core aspects of coaching are to address three key questions:

- Where are you now?
- Where would you like to be?
- How will you achieve this?

Without appropriate and clear goal setting you are simply having a conversation rather than a coaching conversation. As you reflect on your coaching both during and after a session, ask yourself:

*'Is what I'm doing helping the coachee to achieve **his/her** goal?'*

Whose goals?

Effective coaching recognises that goals must belong to the coachee.
As a coach, your role is to facilitate and support your colleagues or your students to their goal achievement. In any learning context motivation and commitment are enhanced through ownership and choice.

However, in performance coaching within a school you will need to accept that the school has an agenda too. This may create tensions between individual and school goals. It is important to be open and honest when addressing this point to maintain the integrity of the coaching process. For example, a colleague may feel that going on a course is the only development option, but the school may be focusing on using internal resources through coaching and mentoring. Often sensitive questioning can provide a way forward.

'In what ways can these ideas work together in this situation?'

Preferred futures

In solution-focused coaching goals are often called **preferred futures**.
The orientation is not only on what things will be like when they have improved, it also emphasises the acceptability to the coachee.

Preferred futures could involve:

- Getting even better at some aspect of your role
- Resolving an issue or difficulty
- Engaging in new developments or challenges

An underlying **preferred future** question in each case could be:

- *'How will you know when this has got even better?'*
- *'What would it be like if the issue were resolved in a way that is useful to you?'*
- *'How will you recognise that things are developing well?'*

Preferred futures

The key element in SF goal setting is eliciting a future-focused and **detailed** description from the coachee of how things **are** (note the tense) in the future **when** they are successful.

The significant benefits of the solution-focused approach to goals are that:

- It builds a sense of hope without which change cannot occur
- It enhances motivation and cooperation
- It generates *specific* descriptions of what **will** be happening
- It leads to questions about when these goals are **already** (maybe partially) happening
- It focuses on strengths and resources needed to achieve change
- The achievement of these behaviours becomes the goal
- The movement towards these goals becomes the rationale for support

Longer-term and interim goals

Longer-term or outcome goals are reflected over the span of the coaching process. They represent the achievement of the preferred future and in that sense are the bigger pictures for change. They are the ultimate success criteria.

Interim goals or targets mark out the steps on the journey to attaining the preferred future. They are descriptions of behaviour and fall within the influence and responsibility of the coachee.

Your role as coach is to help the coachee clarify the goal(s); align interim with outcome goals and to hold the coachee accountable by reviewing progress towards their goals.

Of course, goals may shift during the coaching process as greater insight and understanding around the coaching context unfolds.

Longer-term and interim goals – an example

Teacher R sets as her goal: *'Improving the quality of relationships with my year 9 class'*. The coach then sets about building more detail around this goal:

'Let's imagine it is the end of term and relationships are improved in ways that you want. Describe to me what is different now? What else?'
(See page 55 for more developer questions.)

As a coach you would wish to use questions to 'chunk down' the outcome goal into interim goals which R can directly influence. (Some of the factors involved in achieving the goal will be beyond the direct control of R – the students' responses to R for example.)

Longer-term and interim goals – an example

C: *'So I've got a clear picture of how things will be in the future, R. What would be the first things **you** could do that moved things in that direction?'*

R: *'I suppose I could catch them being good more often and give more praise.'*

C: *'How, **specifically**, will you do this?'*

R: *'I suppose I could welcome them at the door – that would help.'*

C: *'What would the students notice that told them you are even more welcoming?'*

R: *'Well, (pause) smile, say hello, maybe thank them for being on time, that sort of thing?'*

The coach could then explore:

- **How** R would do this, rehearsing behaviours and aligning supportive beliefs
- **When** has she done this before
- **What** benefits emerged from this
- **What** she might notice first in the students' responses, etc

When we set detailed goals positively, we increase our sensitivity to noticing when they fully or partially occur.

Criteria of effective goals

Effective goals should be:

1. **Positive** – what you want rather than what you don't want.
2. **Concrete and observable** – turning feelings into behaviours.
3. **Detailed** – places, times, actions, responsibilities.
4. **Personal** – begin with 'I'.
5. **Multi-sensory** – what does the success look, feel and sound like?
6. **Interactive** – how will achieving X affect Y?
7. **Broad in perspective** – seen through the eyes of others.

Turning concerns into goals

It is quite common for people to be clearer on what they don't want rather than a preferred future. This is often true when working with children. It is possible to take negative statements and reframe them into potential goals.
NB: these will only be **suggestions** to the coachee.

'That class really winds me up and gets me stressed out.'

'So you'd like to find ways to handle the class that allows you to feel calmer more often?'

'I don't like school. The others hit me and won't let me play.'

'Would it help if we found some ways of making friends so you might feel happier at school?'

'Video talk'

We have discussed 'the miracle question' in a previous chapter. Variations that, in our view, are equally effective in setting goals are:

'Imagine you come home from school and you've just had a really good day. What was that like?'

'Suppose we videoed you in this lesson today and again in a couple of weeks when things had improved in the ways you'd like to see.
As we watched them together, how would we tell which video was the most recent? What would be the differences?'

Example questions for colleagues

'When you feel you are being more assertive with the class what are you doing differently?'

'Imagine you are on top of the marking – what other benefits might that bring?'

'When you are building more kinaesthetic learning opportunities into your lessons what will that be like?'

'When your team is pulling together more what will you notice first?'

'You told me that you'd like the opening phase of the lesson to be sharper. I wondered what you feel would be the first thing to hone? How would you recognise that this phase was developing that edge?'

Example questions for children

'What would you like to be different about how you and school get on?'

'Suppose that over the next few weeks school got a little easier to manage – what would that be like?'

'Imagine that tomorrow is a good day. You're at your best and you give it your best shot. So you can be pleased with yourself and the school can be pleased with you. What would you be doing for that to happen?'

'What's your vision of a good future?'

'Let's imagine that being here turns out to be helpful. What will you be doing differently then?'

Example questions for children

'If we made a video of a day when trouble pushed into your life at school and another a short while later when you have learned to resist trouble, what would we see on the second video? How could we tell which is the second video?'

Introduction

 A Solutions
Focus

 Solution-
focused Tools

 Coaching Skills

 Setting Goals

 Developing
Coaching in Your
Own School

 Reflective
Practitioner
Groups

 Further
Information

Developing Coaching in Your Own School

Overview

Having read about the skills and benefits of coaching, the obvious question is: *how does coaching become part of school life?*

Schools are complex and unique organisations. It is beyond the scope of a book this size to explore fully how coaching might develop in your school. Equally, there is no 'one size fits all' approach to coaching in schools. What we offer here are some ideas to stimulate debate and possibilities to consider. In true SF style you could ask:

If coaching is playing a major part in improving the quality of learning in our school what would be happening?

This chapter looks at some different ways in which coaching can be effective and illustrates them with examples from practice. In addition, it introduces a key development idea – the concept of positive deviance – and shows how coaching can build internal capacity by making existing expertise accessible.

Cost or investment?

Schools are fast paced, complex and multi-dimensional environments subject to great pressures and frequently exposed to new initiatives and large volumes of information. How on earth can coaching be developed successfully with everything else going on?

It's worth repeating John Whitmore's definition of coaching:

'Unlocking a person's potential to maximise their performance. It is about helping them learn rather than teaching them.'

Since coaching builds people's capacity to improve, you could actually reverse the question. How on earth can schools effectively continue to improve, make sense of, and integrate new ideas *without* a focus on coaching?

Remember, coaching per se will not bring about school improvement – **high quality** coaching will bring about school improvement.

A touch of realism

Coaching is not a quick fix. Embedding coaching across a school is a process.
It will take time to:

- Establish credibility
- Provide opportunities to train
- Build examples of success which enrol and engage more and more colleagues

However, most people who experience effective coaching comment on the real
benefits and the sense of growth that results.

Nor is coaching the answer to all development issues. Training, performance
management, mentoring, the range of other professional development opportunities
and even competency procedures all have a part to play in bringing about
improvement to working practices.

Some considerations

- Why are we developing coaching? What do we hope to achieve?
- What is our working definition and where does training and mentoring fit?
- Is it a resourced part of our Development Plan?
- Are the SLT **fully** committed *and* involved?
- What style and approach will we adopt?
- How do people become coaches?
- Who becomes a coach – senior staff; anyone; one per department/key stage?
- How are people connected with coaches? Who chooses?
- What notes are kept (if any) and who has access to them?
- Issues of confidentiality
- The environment (physical and emotional) in which coaching occurs
- What resources will we commit?
- How will we recognise the impact of positive coaching?
- How will we inform and celebrate our success?
- How do we extend opportunities for coaching across the school?

Individual coaching – staff

Individual coaching simply means a trained coach, available on request, to support colleagues across the school with individual development issues related to, eg:

- Individual classroom practice
- Leading a team
- Moving into a new role
- Leading new initiatives across the school
- Becoming even better

In this kind of coaching 'contract' the role of the coach is clearly defined and is likely to span an agreed series of sessions.

Having a number of coaches within school offers more scope for coachees to select coaches they feel most comfortable with.

Case study

'As a headteacher a major part of my responsibility is to support my staff and make their jobs as easy as possible. However, as anyone in a senior leadership position will accept, there is a cost. The pressure to respond correctly to a variety of challenges, to make significant decisions on a daily basis is considerable. When a friend who is not a teacher suggested coaching I was unsure. It seemed something that happened in business not education. However, I decided to try it.

*One of the most significant benefits was to have someone **really** listen and remain focused on my needs. I have a strong and supportive team around me and yet this was so different. At first it felt indulgent but it was so valuable.*

*The questions she asked me were incredibly thought-provoking and, because they came from an external perspective, challenged my thinking in new ways. My coach helped me to clarify my goals by encouraging me to describe detailed pictures as if the issues I faced had **already** been solved. We then explored the steps that led me towards my desired solutions.*

Coaching has energised me and I feel my capacity to support others (often using some coaching skills) has been enhanced. I'm a more effective head as a result.'

TF, Headteacher, London.

Individual coaching – children

With children, individual coaching may be used to:

- Improve the effectiveness of learning
- Improve behaviour, coping with emotional challenges or distress
- Improve exam success
- Explore career prospects

Individual coaching – parents

With parents, individual coaching may relate to:

* Collaborative working with the school
* Gaining confidence in managing their child
* Supporting them in developing their child's confidence and self-esteem as a learner

These coaching experiences may be informal or formal, single or multiple sessions. The coaching opportunity may be a natural extension of a class teacher liaising with parents or it may emerge from contact with parents in a more formal role such as SENCO, key stage coordinator, pastoral manager, etc.

Case study A

Context
A year 11 student, readmitted on appeal after permanent exclusion for arson. He experienced emotionally fraught home circumstances and abused drugs and alcohol. Steve, one of the coach/facilitators, explains.

'We met regularly, formally and informally, and I used a solution-focused approach. Exploring what had gone wrong in the past seemed both obvious and pointless. I focused on what he wanted to happen when life at school was more manageable. I used exception questions to uncover how he had kept his temper when things had gone better – they were glimpses of the preferred future. Understanding that he had been successful allowed me to coach him in these successful behaviours so that they became repeated more frequently.

I used scaling (0-10) to identify emotional state and happiness levels and to agree positive behaviours that would bring about improvement to the next step.

Case study A (cont'd)

One particular strategy we found extremely useful was verbally coaching him on a 'miracle walk'. 'Imagine it's summer and you've successfully completed your time here in a way that means teachers can be pleased with you and you can be proud of yourself. Looking back, what did it take to achieve this?' This gave me opportunities to help him identify steps and actions that he was going to take to reach the goals of completing school and accessing college with good qualifications.

The process was not easy. There were highs and lows and many colleagues made a valued contribution to the solutions we were creating.

The boy prepared for his GCSEs and sat them with a focus on achievement. He was extremely grateful and truly recognised that the coaching interventions I had put in place enabled him to reflect on and understand more of the personal resources and qualities that he had to call on which had, up to then, been unrecognised.

For me, too, it was a real achievement. I feel the outcome would not have been possible without the solution-focused coaching approach through which I had enhanced my skills and continue to develop.'

Case study B

'One morning a child arrived in my Yr 1 class with a dummy. When I spoke to the mother at the end of the day about it being inappropriate I was aware it was a sensitive issue which needed tactful handling. However, she became very defensive and conversation became difficult. I sensed she felt her parenting abilities were being questioned, which clearly was not my intention. On reflection, I realised that I had initially addressed the problem rather than sought to explore a solution. When I met up with the mother after the half-term break I made sure I asked a solution-focused question:

"Let's imagine Simon can be in class without his dummy and still feel comfortable and safe, and that you can be confident he is OK. Working together, how can we achieve this?"

The mood shifted and we began to explore collaboratively a common goal. We discussed the steps we could take and the skills we both had to be successful. Although I made suggestions, I spent more time listening and asking questions that moved us towards a solution. For me it was a good illustration of how everyday scenarios can benefit from a shift in our language and approach.'

Jo Boyers, Romford.

Paired coaching

Staff

In paired coaching two colleagues work collaboratively on specific development issues. These could be the same areas explored from different perspectives, eg developing deeper thinking skills in science. Alternatively, each teacher could focus on their own specific development target. The development issues will probably mirror those on page 90 for individual coaching. However, the coaching relationship will be different.

In this model each teacher is both coach and coachee. Development occurs through observation and feedback, either directly or through video examples of the lesson if appropriate, followed by coaching opportunities to reflect on experiences and set new targets.

Students

Many schools have peer mentoring or buddy systems, usually where older children offer support to younger ones in a range of areas.

How would these processes be enhanced by giving children training in solution-focused coaching?

Case Study

'As part of my role as Senior School Improvement Officer I ran small projects in two secondary schools with year 10 and Sixth Form students to develop their skills in solution-focused coaching as part of an anti-bullying programme.

The older students were paired with students lower down the school and worked under the guidance of a teacher. Their role was to support students who experienced bullying. The coaches reported that focusing on exceptions (times when the bullying did not occur or when it troubled them less) was productive. Also, because bullying affects self-esteem, they emphasised compliments and personal resources with the bullied students, building their confidence and resilience.

Students who received the coaching reported it as valuable and supportive. In many cases the bullying stopped, possibly because it was having less impact. There were naturally clear guidelines for when reference should be made to staff but the coaches too felt they had gained from the programme which continues today.'

IM, Oldham LEA.

Three-way coaching cycles

This is variously known as coaching triangles, trios and triads (but not threesomes!) This model offers, in our view, the most effective way of developing coaching **and** coaches across the whole school.

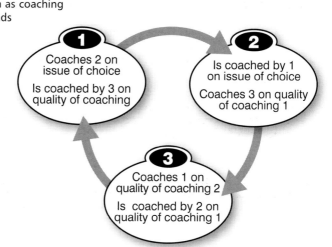

1
Coaches 2 on issue of choice

Is coached by 3 on quality of coaching

2
Is coached by 1 on issue of choice

Coaches 3 on quality of coaching 1

3
Coaches 1 on quality of coaching 2

Is coached by 2 on quality of coaching 1

Three-way coaching cycles

The main advantages of working in threes are:

- Increased levels of support
- Greater opportunities to experience different styles and skills
- Increased commitment
- Receiving focused coaching on your coaching skills

Since there are no 'rules' about how you set up coaching in your school, there are many combinations that can make up the groups of three. Select groupings to fit best with what you want to achieve by developing coaching, especially at the start.

Consider all the possible blends of experience: cross key stage, department, seniority, length of service etc. What grouping would give the most successful and enthusiastic outcomes from which to grow coaching across the school?

Expanding the impact

With paired and triad models, the opportunity arises for each person in the coaching team to 'break away' and set up a new coaching team. This brings more people into the coaching approach and widens the opportunities to use solution-focused language to affect thinking styles and attitudes to development even more positively.

The key point is that development is occurring:

- Internally within the resources of the school
- At a rate and pace that suits individuals
- In a comfortable and non-threatening environment
- With a focus on realistic, relevant and current issues

Because of this a school will be able to:

- Increase its **capacity** for change
- Demonstrate staff ability to **influence** change
- **Embed** valuable changes
- **Sustain** the process of change
- Develop greater **resilience** to external pressures

Positive deviance and unconscious competence

How true of your school are the following statements?

'In every community, organisation or social group, there are individuals whose exceptional behaviours or practices enable them to get better results than their neighbours with the exact same resources.'
Jerry Sternin.

'Most people do not know what their strengths are. When you ask them, they give you a blank stare, or they respond in terms of subject knowledge which is not what you were asking.'
Peter Drucker.

The colleagues and students to whom the first statement applies are known as **'positive deviants.'** And the state of being highly skilled yet largely unaware of *what* you do, *how* you do it and *why* you do it is referred to as **'unconscious competence'**. In our work across hundreds of schools we find most positive deviants fall into this category.

Exploring positive deviance

Whilst the contribution of positive deviants, through their own practice, to the success of the school is considerable, their unconscious competence does mean that this hugely potent body of knowledge – the behaviours, attitudes, values and beliefs that make up successful practice – is unavailable to share across the school.

*Until you become **consciously** aware of things, how can you share them?*

High quality coaching is the most relevant methodology for reconciling the two positions. Consider how some of the benefits of coaching can contribute to a shift towards more conscious awareness of successful practice:

* Increased reflection and insight
* Enhanced perspectives
* Greater self-awareness

Coaching and positive deviance

Becoming more consciously aware expands your options, all of which impact directly on the school as a learning organisation:

Awareness

Change something and become even better

Amplify success – do more of what works

Teach/coach others

Once coaching has facilitated the development of awareness and conscious understanding with positive deviants, they can become a major resource to the organisation.

Using positive deviance

Organisational and culture change, however, is not about a simple transfer of knowledge; it is about changing *behaviours*.

Conventional wisdom would take positively deviant knowledge and attempt to transfer it elsewhere. Our **model of coaching** goes beyond this. It seeks to create sustainable, embedded change by creating interventions or opportunities that encourage people to practise new behaviours. For example:

- Involvement in reflective practice sessions or team reviews (see pages 107-122)
- Participation in a solution-focused coaching programme
- Shadowing a consciously competent positive deviant with the experience enhanced through subsequent coaching
- Joint planning and team-teaching

A summary

Tapping into and amplifying existing success is at the heart of a solution-focused approach and is the platform for sustained school improvement. Combining coaching and positive deviance models is successful because:

- Understanding and knowledge remain *within* the organisation
- Successes can be tracked and publicised more easily
- It builds curiosity – a precursor to all learning
- It proves change comes from doing things differently
- It positively affects confidence in the potential for change
- Motivation and commitment are enhanced by collaboration
- It is about how we already do things so will be met with less internal resistance

Reflective Practitioner Groups

Connecting coaching and reflection

A reflective practice (RP) group simply consists of a group of colleagues engaging in structured discussion about the practice of teaching and learning. They differ from other meetings and discussions because they follow specific formats called **protocols** and they are also **facilitated**.

The links between coaching and RP occur through this facilitation. The questioning skills that generate reflection and new ways of looking at ideas which are at the heart of a coaching conversation are equally valuable when used to explore new thinking and the sharing of good practice within an RP group in schools.

RP groups can be easily incorporated into existing structures such as key stage or departmental meetings.

Case study

Once a month at Higher Side Community School in Knowsley a group of staff who are designated Lead Learners meet as a reflective group. They use the meetings as a discussion forum with group members taking turns at presenting an example of their practice.

Each member takes a turn at leading the meeting and using coaching skills to facilitate the discussions and draw out thinking around the example presented. Interesting ideas that emerge are then discussed with a view to how they can be developed back in their own departments. In this way good practice is explored and remodelled into different areas of the school.

Why reflect?

If specific time and clear structures are provided to promote the professional growth of adults in school, then the learning of children will benefit and improve. RP groups are underpinned by these beliefs:

- Adults in schools working together can make real and lasting improvements to their own organisations and benefit from the sense of collegiality
- Professionals helping each other will more easily turn educational theory into practice and turn targets into real learning outcomes
- The key to school improvement is the development of genuine 'learning communities'
- A huge amount of skill and knowledge exists in schools but is often untapped. Reflective practice provides an effective and stimulating way of tapping into and sharing that knowledge

The facilitator's role

Experience suggests that groups of between four and ten staff who commit to meet regularly throughout the school year work best. It is essential that the group has a facilitator. It is common for group members to rotate the role of facilitator among them. The facilitator has four key roles:

1. To plan the work of the group in order to maintain its focus on improvements in learning outcomes.
2. To use a variety of strategies to generate collaboration, reflection and creativity.
3. When necessary, to deal effectively with conflict and disagreement arising from:
   – Differing expectations of students
   – Contradictory beliefs about what successful teaching is like
   – Challenging school 'norms' and traditions
4. To act as timekeeper and recorder.

Clearly the coaching skills described earlier are highly relevant and support the facilitator's role.

The use of protocols

A protocol consists of a set of structured guidelines for conversation which have been agreed by the group. The advantages of using protocols are that they:

- Provide the arena for building the skills and group culture and, most importantly, the trust necessary for effective collaborative work
- Offer collegial support without criticism
- Make it safe to ask challenging questions of each other
- Give effective ways to make the most of limited time
- Build a space for listening, and often give people a licence just to listen, without having to continually respond
- Ensure that there is some fairness and equality in terms of how each person's issues are addressed.
- Enable existing traditions and norms to be challenged constructively

RP group protocols

The following pages contain some group protocols that can be used by facilitators to help their RP group achieve its objectives. Some of them we have learnt from groups we have supported, others are our adaptations of the work of the Critical Friends Groups operating as part of the Essential Schools Network in the USA.

Each protocol suggests both an order of events and timescales for each part. These are based on our experience of what works well in running such groups but can obviously be shaped to suit your context. As with coaching, a good facilitator 'tunes in' to their group and can sense when it is beneficial to let a conversation run on or to refocus it onto the next stage

RP groups evolve over time and, whilst some of these protocols will become firmly established elements of the group's routines, others will prove less effective within the group's emergent style.

However, the most important thing to remember is that the point is not to 'do' the protocol well, but to have an in-depth, insightful and developmental conversation.

Getting started

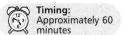
Timing:
Approximately 60 minutes

Setting the scene for the success of the group presents a great chance to integrate SF coaching and facilitation dialogues from the start.

1. Reflect on this individually. *"It is now six months from today, your RP group is functioning as well as you can imagine. What is happening?"* Make notes / pictures / mindmaps etc to capture what it is about the practice that makes it so successful. (7 minutes)

2. In groups of four, take turns to share your 'RP best practice' and why it is so successful. After each turn, the group of four discusses how this practice is different from other school practices. (25 minutes)

3. The whole group re-forms and discusses what the learning was and what the implications are for how the RP group should begin to work. (15 minutes)

4. Debrief the protocol and write four key 'RP Best Practice Headlines' on a large piece of paper. (5 minutes)

Paper talk

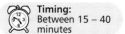

Timing:
Between 15 – 40 minutes

Paper talk can be a gentle, silent reflection or a rapid, but silent, exchanging of ideas. Among its many uses, it has been known to give new insights into complicated problems, get a new development planned, or be the starting point for a structured group discussion. It can also provide powerful affirmation of the creativity and knowledge of the group.

Materials needed – a large sheet of paper on a table and a range of fine-tipped coloured pens.

1. The facilitator explains VERY BRIEFLY that paper talk is a silent activity. No one may talk at all but anyone may add to the paper talk as they please. You can comment on other people's ideas simply by drawing a connecting line to the comment.

2. The facilitator writes a relevant question in a circle in the middle. The question is designed to begin the group's thinking around an issue they all want to examine.

3. The facilitator hands a pen to everyone and invites people to contribute ideas, questions, or statements related to the central question.

Paper talk (cont'd)

4. There is no set sequence or order to the contributions – people write as they feel moved. There are frequently long silences – that is natural. Allow plenty of waiting time.

5. The facilitator can choose how to interact with the group, either simply letting it flow or intervening by:
   - Circling other interesting ideas, and hence inviting comments
   - Writing questions about a participant's comment
   - Adding their own reflections or ideas
   - Connecting two comments together with a line and adding a question mark

6. Before closure, the facilitator invites the group to discuss what has been written on the sheet. (10 minutes)

Support without advice

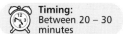

Timing:
Between 20 – 30
minutes

This protocol is designed to help expand the presenter's thinking about an issue that they feel 'stuck' on and for which they need to find alternative routes towards a solution – it is **not** about giving advice. When the group is first introduced to it, they may find it strange or artificial. After their first try they will see the power and usefulness of this deceptively simple protocol. Once established, this protocol doesn't need a facilitator but it is important that participants stick fairly strictly to the timings.

By missing out step 4, this protocol can be extremely successful as a strategy for two experienced practitioners to support the less experienced, as the person presenting can simply listen to a range of possibilities without having to comment.

Support without advice (cont'd)

1. B & C sit facing A. 'A' presents an issue they feel they are stuck on. B & C are silent except to ask questions to keep A talking. (5 minutes)

2. B & C ask clarifying questions to deepen their understanding. (3 minutes)

3. B & C turn to face each other so that A can hear but isn't engaged in the conversation. B & C discuss what they've heard whilst A is silent. (8 minutes)

   • What seem to be the primary issues?
   • What questions does the sticky situation raise for you?
   • What have you tried in similar circumstances?
   • What didn't you hear that you wonder about?

4. A, B & C debrief on the new insights. (4 minutes)

NB It is important that B & C do not ask 'why didn't you?' -type questions of A in phase 2. Equally, phase 3 is not about giving A advice but about exploring their perceptions and experiences around the issue.

Refining practice

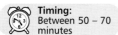

Timing:
Between 50 – 70 minutes

This protocol is a structured way of getting feedback on elements of your practice. It may focus on a child's work, the development of policy or aspects of curriculum development. The process can be as short as 50 minutes.

1. **Introduction phase:** The facilitator briefly introduces the protocol including phases and timings. The presenter brings any work in progress to the group for support. It can be a sample of student work in progress, finished student work that a teacher wishes to examine, a faculty first draft of a policy, etc... (5 minutes)

2. **Presentation phase:** The group read or view the work. The presenter presents the work to the group, elaborating on what has already been given to them. No interruptions or questions are allowed, just listening and note-taking by the group. The presenter may ask for specific feedback or may leave it open for the group to comment as they see fit. (10 minutes)

3. **Clarifying phase:** Group members may ask clarifying questions, but no discussion is allowed. (5 minutes)

Refining practice (cont'd)

4. **Discussion phase:** The group discusses the work together whilst the presenter listens but doesn't comment. (10 minutes)

5. **Feedback phase:** The facilitator asks the group to give the presenter feedback. First the facilitator asks for positive points (5-10 minutes) and then for 'curious' feedback, ie questions that arise, gaps and doubts the group have identified (5-10 minutes). It's important that the facilitator ensures that the feedback is directly related to the work discussed and doesn't refer to the presenter.

6. **Reflection phase:** The presenter responds to the feedback given by the group. Responses should be about changes that might be made, new insights, and clarifications. This is not an opportunity to defend the work. (10 minutes)

7. **Debrief phase:** The facilitator leads a brief conversation about the group's observation of the process. (5-10 minutes)

Constructive group support

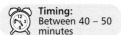

Timing:
Between 40 – 50 minutes

This protocol provides a clear structure for RP groups to work collaboratively and support a group member (the presenter) in closely reflecting on an issue involving a student or another aspect of their work.

1. **Describing phase:** The presenter describes the issues that they'd like the group to support them in thinking through. They may show or distribute examples of the student's work or other documents if they feel it is relevant to facilitating the group's understanding. (7 minutes)

2. **Reflecting phase:** The facilitator then asks the group, *'What are your initial thoughts?'* Group members provide answers without attempting to make judgements about the presenter or their issues. If judgements do emerge, the facilitator can ask for the person to describe the evidence on which their judgement is based. The presenter simply listens without comment. (10 minutes)

Constructive group support (cont'd)

3. **Questioning phase:** The facilitator then asks the group, *'What questions does this suggest to you?'* Members ask any *factual* questions they have, to help them clarify the issue further. The presenter attempts to answer these questions as honestly as they can although they may not yet have an answer. (5-10 minutes)

4. **Speculating phase:** The facilitator then asks the group, *'What are your thoughts?'* Members discuss the issue among themselves. The group may make suggestions about the problems or issues that the presenter has brought to them. The presenter listens and takes notes without joining in. (5-10 minutes)

5. **Insights phase:** It is now the presenter's turn. The presenter offers their perspective on the issues and questions raised. Most importantly, the presenter also comments on any surprising or unexpected things that they heard during the describing, reflecting, questioning and speculating phases. (10 minutes)

6. **Debriefing phase:** Everyone debriefs the process and the new insights generated by the collaborative assessment. (5 minutes)

Further
Information

Choosing training

If you've ever had a speaker on INSET days who demotivated staff, or been on a course that wasn't worth the money, you'll appreciate how crucial getting **quality training** is on such a vital whole-school development issue.

Here is a checklist to help. The trainer should:

✓ Be qualified as a coach themselves

✓ Offer accredited programmes leading to qualifications if desired

✓ Let you talk to previous clients

✓ Have extensive **educational** experience and understand the reality of schools

✓ Work in a solution-focused way

✓ Have experience of coaching beyond education as well

✓ Design an intervention unique to your needs

✓ Ask you what **you** want to achieve and agree success criteria

✓ Keep things simple and jargon free

✓ Be able to talk about their own professional development

Next steps

We hope this book has whetted your appetite for the possibilities and value coaching offers for school and individual improvement. If you have responsibility for the development of others or you are curious as to how your own potential and career is enhanced through powerful learning conversations, you will probably be considering your options.

Whether you just wish to deepen your skills or go further and obtain an accredited Diploma in coaching, the authors offer a range of high quality programmes tailored directly to your specific needs. For further details contact

Munro Training Services Ltd
Tel: 01732 364929
Email: info@munrotraining.co.uk

and

The Critical Difference Ltd
Tel: 01706 645004
Email: peter@thecriticaldifference.biz

Recommended reading and acknowledgements

Coaching for Performance
by John Whitmore
(Nicholas Brealey, 1992)

Coaching in Schools
by Mike Hughes
(Jigsaw Pieces, 2004)

Effective Coaching
by Miles Downey
(TEXERE, New York, 2003)

Solution-focused Coaching
by Green & Grant
(Pearson Education, 2003)

The Coaching Manual
by Julie Starr
(Prentice Hall, 2003)

The Solutions Focus
by Jackson & McKergow
(Nicholas Brealey, 2002)

We would like to acknowledge the amazingly supportive and valuable feedback we have received during our coach training programmes and from the major projects with LAs and other public sector organisations. Our own growth as coaches and our understanding and insights into what is an incredibly powerful way of holding conversations at all levels would not have been possible without you. Thank you

We would also like to acknowledge the Coalition of Essential Schools and the National School Reform Faculty in the USA as contributors to the work on reflective practice and thank them for permission to use and adapt their ideas.

About the authors

Andy Vass

Ian McPhail

Peter Hook

Andy, **Ian** and **Peter** have worked together for many years, pioneering the application of solution-focused approaches to coaching and leadership development. Between them they have established a national reputation for providing high-impact coach training with specific relevance to an educational context. They were recently invited to present their work on 'positive deviance' and solution-focused change in schools to the European Mentoring & Coaching Council conference.

For information about their personal training or consultancy programmes they may be contacted at:

Andy Vass: andy@andyvass.net
Ian McPhail: ian@mcphail.wanadoo.co.uk
Peter Hook: peter@thecriticaldifference.biz

Websites of interest:
www.thecriticaldifference.biz   www.essentialschools.org
www.munrotraining.co.uk   www.mindfields.org.uk
www.thesolutionsfocus.com

Order Form

Your details

Name _____

Position _____

School _____

Address _____

_____

_____

Telephone _____

Fax _____

E-mail _____

VAT No. (EC only) _____

Your Order Ref _____

Please send me:

		No. copies
Coaching & Reflecting	Pocketbook	☐
_____	Pocketbook	☐
_____	Pocketbook	☐
_____	Pocketbook	☐
_____	Pocketbook	☐

Order by Post
Teachers' Pocketbooks
Laurel House, Station Approach
Alresford, Hants. SO24 9JH UK

Order by Phone, Fax or Internet
Telephone: +44 (0)1962 735573
Facsimile: +44 (0)1962 733637
E-mail: sales@teacherspocketbooks.co.uk
Web: www.teacherspocketbooks.co.uk